MEAT
FROM THE FARM TO YOUR TABLE

HEATHER HASAN

rosen publishing's
rosen central

New York

To my son Elijah Abraham: You are truly a gift from God.

Published in 2013 by The Rosen Publishing Group, Inc.
29 East 21st Street, New York, NY 10010

Library of Congress Cataloging-in-Publication Data

Hasan, Heather.
Meat: from the farm to your table/Heather Hasan.— 1st ed.
    p. cm.—(The truth about the food supply)
Includes bibliographical references and index.
ISBN 978-1-4488-6797-4 (library binding)
1. Meat—Juvenile literature. 2. Meat industry and trade—Juvenile literature. I. Title.
TX371.H37 2013
641.3'6—dc23

2011041237

Manufactured in the United States

CPSIA Compliance Information: Batch #S12YA: For further information, contact Rosen Publishing, New York, New York, at 1-800-237-9932.

CONTENTS

I n January 1993, doctors in Seattle, Washington, began noticing that an unusual number of children were being admitted to the hospital with complaints of bloody diarrhea. Health officials were soon able to trace the cases back to undercooked hamburger meat from a chain of local restaurants. Tests of the hamburger patties from these restaurants confirmed that the meat was contaminated with *E. coli* O157:H7 bacteria. (Enterohemorrhagic *Escherichia coli* [EHEC], including the strain *E. coli* O157:H7, are foodborne microorganisms [bacteria] that live in the intestines of humans and other warm-blooded

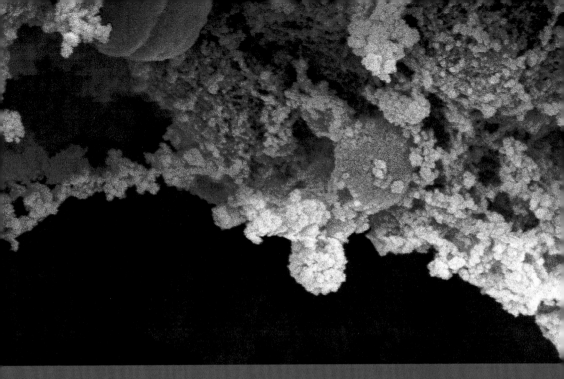

This image, taken with a scanning electron microscope, shows undercooked beef that is contaminated with *E. coli.*

animals.) In most cases, when a person is infected with this bacteria, he or she will suffer from severe stomach cramps; watery, then bloody, diarrhea; and, sometimes, vomiting and fever. At times, *E. coli* O157:H7 causes more life-threatening conditions, such as internal bleeding, kidney failure, and destruction of vital organs. It can also cause seizures, strokes, and nerve damage. Some people (usually young children or elderly people) infected with *E. coli* O157:H7 do not survive.

One of the first children to become sick from the tainted chain-restaurant beef was a six-year-old. The week before Christmas, she ate a hamburger at one of the chain restaurants in San Diego, California. On Christmas Eve, she was admitted to the hospital.

She suffered with terrible pain, had three heart attacks, and died in her mother's arms four days later.

Decades ago, some herds of cattle may have been infected with *E. coli* O157:H7. Yet, this tainted beef would have been distributed only locally, probably infecting just a small group of people. However, most of today's farms are not the same green pastures that they used to be. They are large industrial facilities that produce food in huge amounts. This recent change to the way that livestock are raised, slaughtered, and processed has created conditions that could make an outbreak of harmful bacteria much more widespread, potentially sickening millions of people. In this case, the tainted meat that led to the hospitalization of more than two hundred people and the deaths of four came from only one meat-processing plant. It was distributed to only one particular chain of restaurants, and yet it caused illness in more than seven hundred people in at least four states along the West Coast.

This book will discuss the meat you eat, from how the livestock it comes from are raised and slaughtered to how the resulting meat is processed. It will also include information about the possible harm this system may have on animal welfare, human health, and the environment, and the steps that are being taken to make eating meat as safe as possible.

MEAT AS FOOD AND INDUSTRY

M eat is a nutritious food. It is a rich source of iron, protein, and B vitamins. Meat is the flesh of animals such as pigs, cattle, goats, and lambs that have been raised and prepared for people to eat. The flesh that people think of as meat is mostly the skeletal muscle tissue of these animals. Skeletal muscles make up about 50 percent of an animal's body weight. When an animal is living, its skeletal muscles serve to move and support its skeleton.

WHAT IS MEAT?

Meat can be broadly classified as "red" or "white," depending on how much myoglobin is found in the animal's muscles. Myoglobin is an iron- and oxygen-binding protein that is found in muscle tissue. When myoglobin is exposed to oxygen, it binds to it and makes the meat look red. The meat of mammals such as cattle, sheep, goats, hogs or pigs, and horses is generally considered red, while the meat of chickens and turkeys is considered white. This book will focus on the meat produced from sheep, goats, cattle, and pigs.

Chicken, beef, pork, lamb, and fish are popular types of meat. Other alternatives include venison (deer), ostrich, elk, emu, and bison.

Sheep provide humans with lamb, mutton, and hogget—three types of meat that supply many essential vitamins and proteins. Lamb is the meat from a sheep that is less than one year old. Hogget is the meat of an animal that is between one and two years old. Mutton is the meat from a sheep that is older than two years. Lamb meat is one of the richest sources of conjugated linoleic acid (CLA), which builds muscle and fights cancer. Meat from sheep is very popular in places like the Middle East, India, North Africa, and parts of Europe. However, it accounts for only about 6 percent of the world's meat consumption.

Goat meat is one of the most widely consumed meats in the world. It is most popular in Central and South America, Asia, and Africa, and is considered a delicacy in some European countries. Though most Americans have never tried goat meat, it has slowly been gaining popularity in the United States. Goat meat is easier to digest than some other types of meat. It is also relatively low in fat and cholesterol.

Full-grown cattle provide people with beef. Beef accounts for about 32 percent of the world's meat consumption. Meat from cattle is processed into many different products, including steaks, roasts, hamburgers, veal, and beef sausages. According to the U.S. Department of Agriculture (USDA), Americans eat an average of 60 pounds (27 kilograms) of beef every year. Veal is the meat from a calf that is usually less than three months old when slaughtered. Veal is a pale pink and contains more cholesterol than beef.

Pork, the meat derived from pigs (hogs or swine), is the most widely consumed meat in the world. It accounts for 40 percent of the world's meat consumption. The popularity of pork may be due to its low cost. Choice cuts of pork are much cheaper to buy than similar cuts of lamb or beef. People eat many different pork products, including sausage, bacon, pork chops, and ham.

THE HISTORY OF THE MEAT INDUSTRY

Meat has been a major part of the human diet from the earliest times. Throughout history, the amount of meat that a people or nation eats has shown how well that people or nation is doing economically. As people develop their industries and improve their economic success, they consume more meat.

The meat industry in America had its beginnings in colonial times, when butchers slaughtered and dressed animals for

BELGIAN BLUES

Agricultural scientists have found that meat can be produced more effectively when certain desirable traits are chosen in livestock. An animal's traits are determined by its genes, its recipe for life. Choosing what genes an animal will have is called genetic engineering. In the case of Belgian Blue cattle, the desired trait is large muscle mass. There is a gene that controls the growth of muscle in cattle. Belgian Blues have been genetically engineered to contain a copy of this gene that does not work. This process results in cattle that grow extremely large muscles, providing more beef for the meat industry.

people other than their immediate family members. The first meat-processing plants were located in major cities such as Omaha, Nebraska; Kansas City, Missouri; and Chicago, Illinois. In the early twentieth century, livestock was raised in the rural Midwest and shipped by train to cities where they would be slaughtered and distributed to local butcher shops. After World War II (1939–1945), the technology that was needed to ship refrigerated foods was developed and improved upon. This technology allowed meat-processing plants to move out of the cities and be near where the animals were being raised. Instead of the hassle of moving live animals in railcars, people had the ability to ship animal carcasses where they needed to go. An increase in the demand for meat led to the rise of factory farms.

MEETING THE DEMAND

Even though the USDA suggests that people eat a lot of vegetables, fruits, and whole grains (http://www.choosemyplate.gov), the average American consumes an excessive half a pound (227 grams) of meat per day. To satisfy this huge demand for meat, ten billion animals must be raised and slaughtered each year, according to the Farm Animal Rights Movement. This is an enormous number of animals. To house all of them, factory farms, also known as

Shipping butchered meat to where it is needed is much easier than transporting the live animals.

concentrated animal feeding operations (CAFOs), were created. Factory farms have mainly replaced traditional, more natural farm settings because they are able to produce a lot of meat at a low cost. Factory farming began in the 1920s, soon after the discovery of vitamins A and D. Agricultural scientists believed that if these vitamins were added to livestock feed, the animals would be able to grow without exercise and sunlight. This benefit allowed farmers to raise large numbers of animals indoors year-round.

This meat processing plant in Greeley, Colorado, is getting ready to slaughter, process, and distribute a herd of cattle.

Enclosed buildings overcame most weather problems, kept the animals safe from predators, and made it possible for farmers to easily care for a multitude of animals. Consumers have factory farms to thank for the low cost and availability of meat. Beef, for example, now costs half of what it did in 1970. Nevertheless, many believe that this new system is inhumane to animals and may have created new health risks for consumers.

10 GREAT QUESTIONS
TO ASK A NUTRITIONIST

1. Should I avoid all meat?

2. How often should I eat red meat?

3. What kind of meat is the healthiest?

4. Is it safe to eat raw meat?

5. Are soy products a good alternative to meat?

6. What precautions should I take when handling raw meat?

7. Why is thorough cooking so important for ground products such as hamburger?

8. What meat is best for digestion?

9. What nutrients do I get from meat?

10. Is it healthier to eat meat or to be a vegetarian?

CHAPTER 2

FACTORY FARMS

A feedlot is an animal feeding operation that is used in factory farming for "finishing" livestock. "Finishing" is the word that describes the time in which livestock are fattened prior to slaughtering. Cattle are usually raised on pasture from birth until they are approximately six to eight months old and weigh about 500 to 600 pounds (227 to 272 kg). Most are then shipped to feedlots. There, they will be fattened until they reach market weight, which is about 1,100 to 1,250 pounds (499 to 567 kg). Finishing usually takes about 90 to 120 days. Lambs are nursed by their mothers, and, when they are weaned, begin feeding on pasture or

Pregnant pigs are in small metal cages, where they will be confined until they are ready to give birth.

coarsely ground grain. In the United States, some sheep operations (found mostly in the western states) finish their sheep on pasturelands, while others finish them in feedlots. Before the 1960s, most pigs in the United States were raised in outside lots or pastures. Today, however, more than 90 percent of pigs being raised for pork products are confined indoors for their entire lives.

THE LIVES OF FACTORY FARM ANIMALS

Feedlots are very crowded, filthy, and contain dangerous fumes from animal waste. Many animals confined in feedlots do not even have room to turn around. It is not uncommon for a feedlot in the United States to house as many as one hundred thousand cattle or more than ten thousand pigs in a single location. Pregnant pigs are kept in metal cages not much bigger than themselves, with no nesting material. To create veal, young calves are confined to small wooden crates in which they virtually have no room to move.

Most feedlot floors are made of wire or metal mesh so that manure and urine can drop into a storage container beneath the floor. The waste then flows down into liquefied manure systems, or lagoon systems. Although they are efficient for the farmers, these types of floors can cause hoof and leg problems for the livestock.

Animals in feedlots often show visible signs of stress and hostility. The emotional stress is most likely caused by their inability to do what comes naturally to them. For pigs, this includes behaviors such as rooting (pushing through dirt with their noses) and

Housing for cattle in feedlots varies, depending upon the climate of the area. This feedlot in California is an open lot but offers shade for the animals.

wallowing (rolling in the mud). Animals in factory farms shake their heads for hours on end, bite the bars that contain them, and bite other animals or even themselves. Often, pigs and cattle in these situations will chew the tails of other animals. To keep this biting from happening, the tails and teeth of piglets are often clipped and the tails of cattle are snipped off. Cattle also have their horns cut off or chemically removed. Both cattle and pigs are also usually neutered or spayed to make them more cooperative. For identification purposes, cattle are branded with a hot iron and piglets may have their ears notched. All of this treatment occurs without the aid of painkillers. Many of the procedures leave the animals with lasting pain or discomfort and can lead to infection.

USDA studies show that livestock under extreme stress also have an increased chance of developing and spreading disease. Animals raised for food do receive some protection under state anticruelty laws, but the regulation of their treatment is mainly left to the farm industry itself.

HOW FACTORY FARMS AFFECT THE ENVIRONMENT

Waste from factory farms collects in enormous cesspools, called lagoons, which can cover as much as 120,000 square feet (11,148

This aerial view shows the finishing barns of a factory farm in Missouri. The rectangular lagoons behind the barns hold the animals' waste.

square meters). Theses lagoons are filled with waste matter, bacteria, chemicals and drugs, and blood. Studies have shown that such lagoons release hundreds of dangerous gases into the surrounding air. Research has shown that breathing in these gases can cause asthma, bronchitis, headaches, depression, diarrhea, rapid heartbeats, and brain damage in humans.

As noted by Jennifer Sandy, a program officer for the National Trust for Historic Preservation, factory farms produce about 1.4 billion tons (1.3 billion metric tons) of sewage each year in the United States. That is 130 times the amount of human waste that is produced! Hundreds of millions of pounds of this animal sewage are then dumped on land where runoff takes it to rivers and lakes across the country. During times of heavy rain, pig lagoons have also been known to overflow, contaminating nearby sources of human drinking water.

To keep situations like these from occurring, most feedlots need a permit from the government before they can operate. To receive a permit, feedlot operators must prove that they have a plan for disposing of feedlot waste. The Environmental Protection Agency (EPA) also has authority under the Clean Water Act to regulate the management of animal waste on factory farms in the United States.

PEOPLE ARE WHAT THEIR FOOD EATS

The crowded conditions of factory farms, along with the dust, dirt, and toxic gases from animal waste, create an unsanitary environment for the animals. In these conditions, it is more likely that illnesses such as cholera, pneumonia, trichinosis, and dysentery will spread rapidly from one animal to the next. These diseases would kill most of the animals in feedlots if it weren't for antibiotics.

In the United States, 29 million pounds (13.2 million kg) of antibiotics are added to animal feed each year, according to the Food and Drug Administration (FDA). In fact, 80 percent of the antibiotics produced in this country are used in animal industries. They are added to prevent and heal sickness but also to help animals grow. If not for these antibiotics, an animal's growth would suffer because of the amount of energy it takes to fight off disease in the crowded, unsanitary conditions.

What farm animals are fed, what drugs they are given, and

SUSTAINABLE FARMS—A GOOD ALTERNATIVE

For people who are concerned about eating meat that comes from factory farms, sustainable farming may be a good alternative. Sustainable farming is a way of raising livestock for food that is humane to animals, healthy for consumers, and does not harm the environment. Sustainable farms try to put back into the environment what they take out so that it will be there for future generations. Animals at sustainable farms are allowed to carry out their natural behaviors, such as rooting and grazing. They are fed a natural diet. Many sustainable farms do not use chemicals of any kind, although some use pesticides sparingly.

the conditions in which they are raised significantly affect the health of the humans who eat them. The agencies responsible for the safety of food products in the United States are the USDA and the FDA. (The Canadian Food Inspection Agency safeguards food, animals, and plants in Canada.) The FDA has the authority to control what goes into animal feeds and drugs. It attempts to keep antibiotics out of the human food supply by requiring that an animal not be slaughtered until the antibiotics have been given time to wear off. The USDA then randomly samples meat from slaughtered livestock to check for traces of antibiotics in the meat. Despite these precautions, some still fear that small amounts of these antibiotics could end up in meat that is consumed by humans. If a lot of meat is eaten, the antibiotics could build up in a person's body. According to Dr. Robert Lawrence, director of the Johns Hopkins Center for a Livable Future, some of the antibiotics that doctors use to treat human illness may no longer be effective at fighting disease because of the overuse of these antibiotics.

In nature, cattle and sheep eat grass and pigs eat mainly grass, worms, and insects. However, in a factory farm, these animals are fed an unnatural diet of mostly cheap corn and soy. This feed cuts costs and fattens animals up in a shorter period of time. In addition to this feed, animals in feedlots may also be fed appetite stimulants and pesticides, herbicides, growth hormones, arsenic, and waste from other animals. It is not uncommon for cattle to be fed whatever is found on the floor of chicken coops. This food includes chicken feed, feathers, and manure.

USDA meat inspectors visit a meat processing plant in Nebraska to check quality control procedures and safety.

Some scientists fear that the chemicals being fed to livestock could end up in the meat being eaten by humans. Hormones are chemicals that are produced naturally in all mammals, including humans. Still, some researchers believe that the hormones given to livestock to make them gain weight faster could affect the age of puberty for girls. A journal article published in *Public Health Nutrition* in 2010 showed that girls who ate a high-meat diet went through an earlier puberty. Early puberty in girls has been linked to both cancer and heart disease. Currently, federal law allows hormones to be given to cattle and sheep but not to

USDA officials seized these sheep from a farm in Vermont, killed them, and tested them for mad cow disease. The sheep may have contracted the disease before they were shipped from Europe.

pigs. The USDA spot-checks meat to make sure that the hormone levels found in it are not higher than allowed by the FDA.

Until 1997, it was acceptable for cattle in America to be fed the remains of other cattle and sheep. It is dangerous for cattle to eat parts of other cattle because of mad cow disease (also known as bovine spongiform encephalopathy, or BSE). Cattle infected with mad cow disease show a change in behavior, lose weight, and develop uncoordinated movements before dying. In 1996, medical researchers realized that humans who ate the meat of these sick animals could also develop BSE. Though feeding cattle parts to other cattle is no longer allowed, it is still OK for feedlots to use parts of cattle in chicken feed. Because cattle are then fed chicken waste (which includes chicken feed), it is possible that cattle could still be eating infected meat from other cattle. Even so, the risk of human infection is thought to be low. In the last twenty years, fewer than two hundred people worldwide have died from the human form of BSE, called Creutzfeldt-Jakob disease.

MYTHS AND FACTS

Myth: Freezing meat kills bacteria.
Fact: Freezing stops the growth of bacteria but does not destroy it. Proper cooking, however, kills most foodborne bacteria.

Myth: Eating red meat will kill you.
Fact: Eating red meat in moderation is not unhealthy for you. Meat provides humans with protein, iron, and natural fats.

Myth: Consumers are more likely to get sick from eating meat today than they were in the past.
Fact: The government has worked to make the meat industry safe for consumers and is continuing to work to this end. Although potential outbreaks of illness could be more widespread than in the past because of the way meats are processed and distributed, processing has become safer than methods in the past.

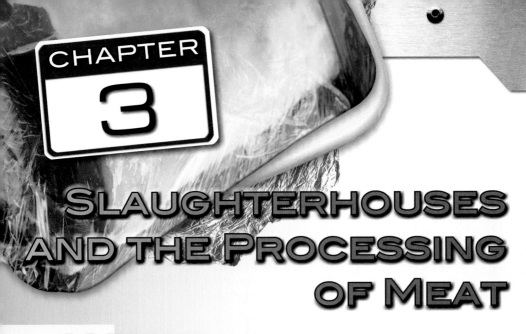

CHAPTER 3

SLAUGHTERHOUSES AND THE PROCESSING OF MEAT

When livestock have grown fat enough, they are loaded into a truck and taken to a slaughterhouse, or meat-processing plant. Once the animals arrive at the slaughterhouse, they are placed in holding pens. Considerable research has been done to make these pens as stress-free as possible for the animals. They then enter the slaughterhouse in single file. When they reach the end, they go through a narrow chute that restrains them for stunning. Stunning is required in the United States by the Humane Slaughter Act of 1958. The typical method for stunning in the United States is a concussion method using a captive bolt stunner. With this method, an air-powered gun shoots a metal rod into the head of the animal, knocking it unconscious. Next, the animal is hung upside-down by its legs. An incision is made, usually to the throat, to make the animal bleed. The animals are left hanging while they bleed to death. They are killed while they are alive (yet unconscious) because it is important that the heart pumps the blood from the body. Extra blood left in the tissue would cause the meat to decompose more quickly, wasting

TEMPLE GRANDIN

Dr. Temple Grandin was born with autism, a developmental disorder that sometimes gives people the ability to intensely focus on certain things, but also leads to isolation and social difficulties. It may have been Grandin's condition that allowed her to view cattle in a unique way and understand their behavior during slaughter. This remarkable perspective led her to design corrals for meat plants in which the cattle walk in single file and sweeping curves, thereby reducing the stress of the animals and making slaughter safer, faster, and less expensive. Today, Grandin's design is used in most U.S. slaughterhouses.

Dr. Temple Grandin, shown here in a corral in Fort Collins, Colorado, has worked to bring humane treatment to farm

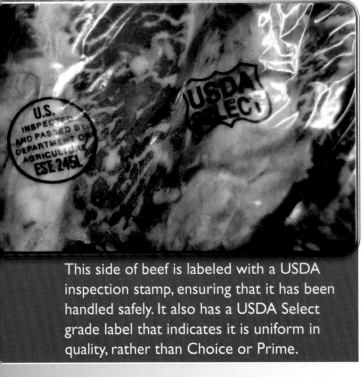

This side of beef is labeled with a USDA inspection stamp, ensuring that it has been handled safely. It also has a USDA Select grade label that indicates it is uniform in quality, rather than Choice or Prime.

the meat. Once an animal has died, it goes through a series of processing stations. For cattle and sheep, these steps include the removal of the hide. Pigs are put through a scalding tank, designed to soften their skin and remove their hair. Animals' internal organs are also removed.

KEEPING SLAUGHTERHOUSES SAFE

The USDA regulates most slaughterhouses in the United States. It requires that the people handling, moving, and stunning the animals treat them humanely and know how to do their jobs properly. It is also required that a veterinarian be on-site at all times. Before animals are slaughtered, they are supposed to be inspected for illness, injury, or disease. In 2003, it was discovered that a downed cow had BSE. As a result of this incident, the USDA approved a policy that no cattle could be slaughtered for human consumption if they are too sick to stand or walk. However, the United States currently tests less than 1 percent of its cattle for BSE before slaughter.

Ideally, the slaughtering process should be carried out as humanely as possible, but things don't always go as they should. Reports have been made of animals being improperly stunned, resulting in animals that were still conscious when their throats were cut or when they went through the scalding tank for hair removal. Handlers have also been found using abusive methods to force downed cattle to walk to slaughter. This violates federal laws designed to prevent BSE and other diseases from entering the human food supply. When inspectors from the USDA uncover violations, they take actions such as suspending a slaughterhouse until changes have been put into practice.

Following slaughter, meat is inspected for wholesomeness either by the USDA or by state systems that have standards equal to the federal government. The animals and their internal organs are checked for signs of disease. To receive a stamp from the USDA on their meat, slaughterhouses must also follow strict sanitation rules. Equipment and tools used for slaughter must be cleaned, sanitized, and disinfected during production. Workers must also practice good hygiene, such as wearing clean clothes and washing their hands.

WHAT DANGERS COULD BE LURKING IN MEAT?

Despite the safety precautions taken in slaughterhouses, some harmful pathogens may still find their way into meat. Pathogens are microorganisms, such as viruses or bacteria, which cause disease. The pathogens that are commonly found

Ground beef is packed at a meat factory. One package of ground beef actually contains a mixture of meat from hundreds of cattle.

in meat include *Escherichia coli* (*E. coli*), *Campylobacter jejuni*, *Trichinella spiralis*, *Salmonella*, *Clostridium perfringens*, and *Listeria monocytogenes*. In the United States, these pathogens cause an estimated 76 million illnesses, 325,000 hospitalizations, and 5,000 deaths each year.

Pathogens from infected animals are spread not only in feedlots, but also in slaughterhouses. In slaughterhouses, most pathogens get into meat during the removal of animal hides and of the animals' digestive systems (the stomach and intestines).

Breakfast meats, such as the sausage being processed here, contain the highest quantity of potentially harmful additives of all meat.

Cattle, sheep, and pigs enter the slaughterhouses smeared and caked with the manure that they have spent most of their lives lying in. Many attempts are made to keep this material out of the food supply, such as cleaning slaughtered meat with chlorine. However, if an animal's hide is not cleaned properly, chucks of dirt and manure could fall into the meat as it is being removed. Likewise, if an animal's digestive tract is not handled properly, what's inside could spill out and contaminate the meat. Although there are rules for keeping the knives and other tools used for slaughtering clean, hurried workers may forget.

The odds of spreading contaminated meat rise sizably when meat is processed into ground products because the meat from hundreds of animals is being ground together. A single infected cow, for instance, could contaminate 32,000 pounds (14,515 kg) of ground beef. The USDA spot-checks slaughterhouses to test for *E. coli*. Because of today's technology, even a small amount of bacteria can be detected. However, many people believe that the frequency of these spot-checks should increase.

IRRADIATION

One way to kill or damage the pathogens in meat is irradiation. Irradiation is the process of passing food through radiation. This process kills much of the bacteria in meat, making it safer to eat. Scientists have been experimenting with irradiation since 1950. In 1985, the FDA approved irradiation on pork to control trichinosis. In 1997, irradiation was approved to control pathogens such as *E. coli* and *Salmonella* in beef, lamb, and pork.

Irradiation does not change the appearance or taste of meat. During irradiation, energy is passed through the food but does not stay in the meat—just as teeth that are X-rayed and food that is microwaved do not hold on to the energy that was passed through them. Nonetheless, irradiation does cause chemical changes in food. It produces substances that are not known to be present in foods that have not been irradiated. These substances have been named "radiolytic products." Scientists believe that these radiolytic products are no more dangerous than the

A scientist and an official from a food processing plant attend a congressional hearing in Washington, D.C., to discuss the safety of irradiation. *Top, left:* This is the radura, the symbol used to label irradiated meats.

chemical substances created by cooking foods, called thermolytic products. Although irradiation is approved by a majority of health institutions, including the World Health Organization (WHO) and the Centers for Disease Control and Prevention (CDC), many organizations remain concerned about its effects.

The FDA regulates what foods irradiation can be used on, at what dose it can be used, and how irradiated products are to be labeled. The USDA is responsible for inspecting and monitoring irradiated meats. The FDA requires that all irradiated products bear a label with an international symbol, called a radura, as well as a statement such as, "Irradiated for your food safety" or "Treated with irradiation to reduce potential for foodborne illness."

PROCESSED MEAT—A CHEMICAL CUISINE

Processed meats are meat products that have longer shelf lives because of preservatives that have been added to them. Some of the more common types of processed meats are deli meats, hot dogs, pepperoni, sausage, and bacon. Fresh meats contain no additives unless otherwise noted on the label. Adding preservatives to meat to keep it from going bad is not a new concept. People have been adding salt to meat for centuries because salt prevents the growth of some types of bacteria that cause meat to spoil.

Today, about 2,800 different additives are used. Food additives are substances that are put into food to improve its color, texture, flavor, or freshness. The FDA and USDA share the responsibility for the safety of food additives. Approved additives are continually reviewed for safety. However, many scientists and consumers question the necessity and safety of many of the ingredients used.

Many chemicals are added to processed meats. Some of these, such as corn syrup and dextrose, simply add empty calories to the meat. However, the additives in processed meats that scientists find most worrisome are nitrites and nitrates. Sodium nitrate (NaNO$_3$) and sodium nitrite (NaNO$_2$) are found in lots of processed meats. Sodium nitrite is added to prevent the growth of bacteria that can lead to foodborne illnesses, preserve products so that they have longer shelf lives, and fix the color in meat. Sodium nitrite makes meat look fresh by turning gray-looking meat red. Sodium nitrate is added to some meat because it slowly turns into nitrite. When meat containing nitrites is heated, the nitrites become nitrosamines. Nitrosamines are chemicals that are known to cause cancer. The USDA has set limits on the amount of sodium nitrite that can be used during meat processing.

WHAT YOU CAN DO

Being educated about where your meat comes from empowers you with the knowledge to make choices about your health and what you value in food. Understanding how factory farms and slaughterhouses work allows you to make educated choices when deciding what to eat and where to buy your food. As a more educated shopper, you will know what to look for and what to avoid.

KNOW YOUR LABELS

The USDA regulates most labeling, so you can trust labels to tell you what is in your food. However, when buying meat, it is important that you know what certain labels mean and what they don't mean. For instance, the term "grass-fed" does not always mean that an animal was spending its days out on the pasture. For meat to receive a USDA grass-fed label, it must come from an animal that has been fed on only its mother's milk and forage (hay, grass, and other greens) during its lifetime. Though the animals could be grazing, they may also be spending their time indoors being fed stored forage.

The USDA's standards for organic meat are fairly strict. In order for meat to be marked "Certified Organic", it must come

The label "Certified Organic" on this beef package implies that the USDA's Food Safety and Inspection Service has evaluated the meat for quality. The meat has 95 percent or more organic content.

from animals that were only fed organic feeds. Organic feeds have at least 80 percent organic ingredients and do not contain antibiotics, slaughterhouse waste, or genetically modified grains. When buying certified organic meat, you can also have some confidence that the animal you are eating had healthy and natural living conditions, such as access to the outdoors, exercise, and bedding. However, the USDA does not specifically say that an animal needs to have access to a pasture to be considered organic. If you want meat from an animal that was raised on a pasture, look for that on the label. If it doesn't say that the animal had access to pasture grazing, you should assume that it didn't. For beef, the term "natural" indicates that the cattle were not given antibiotics or hormones. The label "Antibiotic Free" does not mean much. Although antibiotic-free meat came from an animal that was not continuously fed antibiotics, many companies using this label simply give their animals other antimicrobial drugs. These animals are usually raised on feedlots as well.

For processed meats, such as hot dogs, beware of labels that say "natural" or "no added nitrite." Although sodium nitrite has not been added to these products, they are usually made with celery powder or celery juice, which are naturally high in nitrite. In fact, in 2011, the *Journal of Food Production* published a study that found that these "natural" meats could have up to ten times as much nitrite as meats made with sodium nitrite.

KNOW WHERE YOUR FOOD COMES FROM

Who you buy your food from makes a difference because you support them with your money. Supermarkets are convenient and they are carrying more and more organic food, but they rarely carry food from local, sustainable farms. Most supermarkets and large grocery stores usually carry only meats from animals that were raised on factory farms. Nevertheless, many are including products from local farms, and they often identify them as having come from nearby communities.

If you are looking for non-factory farm foods, your local farmers' market is another option for you. Without too much effort, you should be able to locate one near you. Many local farms and ranches

USDA United States Department of Agriculture
Agricultural Marketing Service

USDA ORGANIC

| Home | About AMS | Online Forms | Help | Contact Us |

You are here: Home / Farmers Markets and Local Food Marketing / Farmers Markets Search

Farmers Markets Search
Accessible version

AMS works to maintain a current listing of farmers markets throughout the United States. Market information included in the National Farmers Market Directory is voluntary and self-reported to AMS by market managers, representatives from state farmers market agencies and associations, and other key market personnel. Listings in the Directory are updated on an ongoing basis throughout the year, and each spring, AMS makes a concentrated effort to solicit new information from farmers market stakeholders. Both a national map of farmers markets (static) and state-specific maps of farmers markets (interactive) are available for viewing. To see a state-specific map, select a state from the select box at the top of the state column below; a link will appear for that state's map. To add or change market information, please contact the AMS Marketing Services Division.

To filter by location enter a zip code and choose a distance, then click search. To filter by market name, enter part or all of a market name in the box above the market name column and press 'Enter'. To filter by products, click the 'Products Available' tab and select individual product categories. Only markets that reported having those product categories will be displayed. To filter by payment method, click the 'Payment Accepted' tab and select payment types. Only markets that reported accepting those payment types will be displayed. To filter by market location, click the 'Market Location' tab and select location types from the options listed in the pull down menu. Only markets that reported their type of market location will be displayed. To see detailed information click the Info window icon next to the market name.

An exportable Excel file of farmers market listings and geographic coordinates is available from data.gov. Please note that the current exportable file of farmers market contact information and geographic coordinates still reflects data from the FY 2010 update. Do check back in October, when new geographic coordinate data from the FY2011 update will be available!

| Search Near | Products Available | Payment Accepted | Market Location | State Contacts |

Search near ZIP: _____ Distance: 5 ▼ miles (search) (clear)

Info	MarketName	City	State	Website
			All ▼	
▢	10:10 Farmers Market	Douglasville	Georgia	↗
▢	100-Mile Market	Kalamazoo	Michigan	↗
▢	10th Street Community Farmers' Market	Lamar	Missouri	
▢	112st Madison Avenue	NY	New York	
▢	14&U Farmers' Market	Washington	District of Columbia	
▢	17 on the Square	Gettysburg	Pennsylvania	
▢	17th Ave Market	Minneapolis	Minnesota	↗
▢	17th Street Farmers Market	Richmond	Virginia	↗
▢	1800 St. Julian Place Farmers Market	Columbia	South Carolina	
▢	2011 Wood County Farmers' Market	Wisconsin Rapids	Wisconsin	

|◄ ◄◄ Page 1 of 723 ►► ►| 10 ▼   View 1 - 10 of 7,222

This USDA Web site (http://search.ams.usda.gov/farmersmarkets) enables consumers to enter their Zip codes to the search engine to find farmers' markets that are located nearby.

WHAT ARE YOU EATING IN YOUR SCHOOL CAFETERIA?

Find out what kind of food is being served in your school cafeteria. If you don't like what you discover, you may want to do some research on Farm to School programs. These programs connect schools to local farms that can supply them with healthy meals to be served in the cafeterias. This fairly new concept improves student nutrition, supports local farmers, and protects the environment. Currently, there are more than two thousand Farm to School programs nationwide. Information on how to start such a program can be found at http://www.farmtoschool.org/howtostart.php.

sell their products at farmers' markets. However, never assume anything about the meat you buy. Always ask about the things that are important to you, such as how the animal was fed and housed, and whether or not antibiotics or hormones were used in raising the animal. The USDA has a search engine (http://search.ams.usda.gov/farmersmarkets/default.aspx) for finding local farmers' markets. You can also find area farmers' markets, as well as sources for other local and sustainable organic goods, at EatWellGuide.org.

If you'd like to know exactly where your food comes from, you and your family can also join a community supported agriculture (CSA) network. With a CSA, you buy shares of what a farm produces. Generally, members of a CSA receive a box of farm products each week. You will know what farms your products are coming from and can even visit them to see how your meat is being raised. CSAs can be found by searching LocalHarvest.org/csa and EatWellGuide.org.

KNOW HOW TO HANDLE AND PREPARE YOUR FOOD

By the time meat reaches the grocery store, members of the meat industry and the government have taken steps to ensure its safety. However, it is important that you take steps to maintain safety all the way to your table. Meat should not be purchased if its package is torn or punctured or if it is past its "sell by" date. Meat should either be frozen or cooked by this date. If you freeze your meat, do not defrost it at room temperature. Keeping meat cold while it's defrosting is important in preventing bacterial growth.

The FDA allows only the use of meat-packaging materials that are thought to not affect the meat or cause harm to the consumer. The USDA warns that you should never heat your meat in the foam-insulated trays or plastic wraps that they come in, however. This could allow the chemicals from the packaging to enter your food and cause you harm.

All raw meats should be cooked to a safe internal temperature. The USDA recommends that all raw beef, pork, veal, and lamb be cooked to an internal temperature of 145°F (63°C) and that ground versions of these meats be cooked to 160°F (71°C) as measured with a food thermometer. After handling raw meat, you should wash anything that came into contact with it, including countertops, knives, cutting boards, and your hands.

This teen shopper is learning how to check meat to ensure that it has been stored at the proper temperature. Meat packages should not be warm to the touch or contain excess liquid.

KNOW HOW YOU CAN ACTIVELY PROMOTE GOOD FARMING PRACTICES

The first step in becoming active in the promotion of good farming practices is to educate yourself. Are there any factory farms in your area? If so, find out who is in charge of regulating them. Also, find out how they are affecting your community. Talk to local government and health officials. You can speak with local officials like town hall members, the mayor, or the district attorney. If there are any family farms nearby, talk to the farmers about agricultural issues in your area. Use the information that you have learned to educate others. Some ideas for how you can get involved in your school and community include the following:

- Ask a local farmer to speak to your class about sustainable farming and humane ways to raise livestock.
- Start a garden at your school. This is a lot of fun, and it will get your classmates and community more interested in agricultural issues.

- Educate your family and friends about factory farming and possible alternatives for meat sources.
- Write a letter to your representatives on the local, state, or national level and voice any concerns you may have about the meat you eat or buy.
- See if your school would be interested in a Farm to School program. If not, try getting just one or two items on the menu changed. Don't be afraid to start small!

These teens show their pigs during a 4-H Swine Showmanship event in Montana. Young people learn about the selection, production, breeding, and management of swine from such programs.

Once you have become educated about the different choices you have when buying your food, you can use that knowledge to really make a difference. Your choices make a difference, not only in your own health but also in the welfare of animals, the condition of the environment, and the strength of your community. You can be an important part of shaping a better meat industry for tomorrow!

GLOSSARY

arsenic A highly poisonous metallic element that is used in killing insects and weeds.

cholesterol A waxy, fatlike substance made by the liver and found in the blood. People also get cholesterol from eating animals.

conjugated linoleic acid (CLA) A trans-fatty acid that has a beneficial health effect and is found in dairy products and meat.

decompose To decay or become rotten.

growth hormone A substance that encourages growth in animal or plant cells.

herbicide A substance that is toxic to plants and is used to destroy unwanted vegetation.

industry A large-scale production.

mammal A class of warm-blooded animals that have, in the female, the ability to feed young through milk-secreting organs.

neuter To remove the sexual organs of a male animal.

pathogen A bacterium, virus, or other microorganism that can cause disease.

pesticide A substance that is used to destroy insects or other things harmful to plants or animals.

spay To sterilize a female animal by removing the ovaries.

sustainable Using natural resources without destroying the ecological balance of an area.

trichinosis A disease cause by trichinae (a worm parasite), usually from infected meat, especially pork, and characterized by digestive problems, fever, and muscular problems.

FOR MORE INFORMATION

Canadian Food Inspection Agency (CFIA)
1400 Merivale Road
Ottawa, ON K1A 0Y9
Canada
(800) 442-2342
Web site: http://www.inspection.gc.ca
The CFIA bolster's Canada's food safety and protects the nation's environment to ensure the health of all Canadians.

Canadian Organic Growers (COG)
323 Chapel Street
Ottawa, ON K1N 7Z2
Canada
(888) 375-7383
Web site: http://www.cog.ca
The COG is a charitable organization whose mission is to lead local and national communities toward sustainable organic stewardship of land, food, and fiber while respecting nature, upholding social justice, and protecting natural resources.

Eatwild
P.O. Box 7321
Tacoma, WA 98417
(866) 453-8489
Web site: http://www.eatwild.com
Eatwild provides information about the benefits of raising animals on pasture. It also provides direct links to local farms that sell all-natural, grass-fed products.

Farm to School
110 Maryland Avenue NE, #307
Washington, DC 20002

(202) 543-8602

Web site: http://www.farmtoschool.org

Farm to School brings healthy foods from local farms to schoolchildren throughout the United States.

U.S. Department of Agriculture (USDA)

1400 Independence Avenue SW

Washington, DC 20250

(202) 720-2791

Web site: http://www.usda.gov

The USDA supports rural development, food safety, nutrition, and research for agricultural technology and publishes information on all aspects of agriculture. For information about its recommendations for healthy eating, see http://www .choosemyplate.gov.

U.S. Food and Drug Administration (FDA)

10903 New Hampshire Avenue

Silver Spring, MD 20993

(888) 463-6332

Web site: http://www.fda.gov

The FDA works to assure that the food supply is safe, wholesome, sanitary, and honestly labeled.

WEB SITES

Due to the changing nature of Internet links, Rosen Publishing has developed an online list of Web sites related to the subject of this book. This site is updated regularly. Please use this link to access the list:

http://www.rosenlinks.com/food/meat

FOR FURTHER READING

Anderson, Judith. *Know the Facts About Diet* (Know the Facts). New York, NY: Rosen Publishing Group, 2010.

Barstow, Cynthia. *The Eco-Foods Guide*. Gabriola Island, BC, Canada: New Society Publishers, 2002.

Bourette, Susan. *Meat: A Love Story*. New York, NY: G. P. Putnam's Sons, 2008.

Cotler, Amy. *The Locavore Way*. North Adams, MA: Storey Publishing, 2009.

Cox, Jeff. *The Organic Food Shopper's Guide*. Hoboken, NJ: John Wiley & Sons, 2008.

Fairlie, Simon. *Meat*. White River Junction, VT: Chelsea Green Publishing Company, 2010.

Green, Emily K. *Meat and Beans*. Minnetonka, MN: Bellwether Media, 2007.

Harmon, Daniel E. *Fish, Meat, and Poultry: Dangers in the Food Supply* (What's in Your Food? Recipe for Disaster). New York, NY: Rosen Publishing Group, 2008.

Niman, Nicolette. *Righteous Porkchop: Finding a Life and Good Food Beyond Factory Farms*. New York, NY: HarperCollins Publishers, 2009.

Planck, Nina. *Real Food: What to Eat and Why*. New York, NY: Bloomsbury, 2006.

Rimas, Andrew. *Beef*. New York, NY: HarperCollins Publishers, 2008.

Schlosser, Eric, and Charles Wilson. *Chew on This. Everything You Don't Want to Know About Fast Food*. New York, NY: Houghton Mifflin, 2007.

Toldra, Fidel. *Handbook of Meat Processing*. Ames, IA: Blackwell Publishing, 2010.

Watson, Stephanie. *Fast Food* (What's in Your Food? Recipe for Disaster). New York, NY: Rosen Publishing Group, 2008.

Watson, Stephanie. *Mystery Meat: Hot Dogs, Sausages, and Lunch Meat* (Incredibly Disgusting Food). New York, NY: Rosen Publishing Group, 2011.

Friend, Catherine. *The Compassionate Carnivore*. Philadelphia, PA: Da Capo Press, 2008.

Iowa State University. "Food Irradiation—What Is It?" June 9, 2010. Retrieved September 15, 2011 (http://www.extension.iastate.edu/foodsafety/irradiation).

Masson, Jeffrey Moussaieff. *The Face on Your Plate*. New York, NY: W. W. Norton & Company, 2009.

McCorkell, Don. *A River of Waste: The Hazardous Truth About Factory Farms*. A Video Documentary. United States: Cinema Libre Distribution, 2009.

National Sustainable Agriculture Coalition. "USDA and FDA Data on Antibiotic Resistance Is Deficient." September 16, 2011. Retrieved October 26, 2011 (http://sustainableagriculture.net/blog/antibiotic_us).

Park, Miyun. *Gristle: From Factory Farms to Food Safety*. New York, NY: The New Press, 2010.

PBS. "Industrial Meat." 2011. Retrieved September 15, 2011 (http://www.pbs.org/wgbh/pages/frontline/shows/meat/industrial/consolidation.html).

Rogers, Imogen S. "Diet Throughout Childhood and Age at Menarche in a Contemporary Cohort of British Girls." *Public Health Nutrition*, Vol. 13, Issue 12, 2010, pp. 2,052–2,063.

Sandy, Jennifer. "Factory Farms: A Bad Choice for Rural America." *Forum Journal*. Vol. 23, No. 2, Winter 2009. Retrieved October 26, 2011 (http://www.preservationnation.org/forum/library/public-articles/factory-farms.html).

Schlosser, Eric. *Fast Food Nation*. New York, NY: Harper Perennial, 2005.

U.S. Department of Agriculture. "Beef...from Farm to Table." May 26, 2011. Retrieved September 15, 2011 (http://www.fsis.usda.gov/factsheets/beef_from_farm_to_table/index.asp).

U.S. Department of Agriculture. "Fresh Pork from Farm to Table." June 21, 2011. Retrieved September 15, 2011 (http://www.fsis.usda.gov/factsheets/pork_from_farm_to_table/index.asp).

U.S. Environmental Protection Agency. "Beef Production." September 10, 2009. Retrieved September 15, 2011 (http://www.epa.gov/agriculture/ag101/beef.html).

U.S. Environmental Protection Agency. "Pork Production." September 10, 2009. Retrieved September 15, 2011 (http://www.epa.gov/agriculture/ag101/pork.html).

Waldman, Murray, M.D. *Dying for a Hamburger*. New York, NY: St. Martin's Press, 2004.

INDEX

About the Author

Heather Hasan has degrees in chemistry and biochemistry. She enjoys eating meat but tries to purchase foods that support her local community of Durham, North Carolina. She also tries to buy foods that are safe and healthy for her family, which includes her husband, Omar, and their children, Samuel, Matthew, Sarah, and Elijah.

Photo Credits

Cover, p. 1 (cow) © www.istockphoto.com/Ziva_K, (packaged meat) © www.istockphoto.com/Ugurhan Betin; cover, pp. 1, 23 (towel) © www.istockphoto.com/milanfoto; pp. 3 (hot dogs), 40 © www.istockphoto.com/Juanmonino; p. 3 (steaks) © www.istockphoto.com/moniaphoto; pp. 4–5 Dr. Gary Gaugler/Photo Researchers, Inc.; pp. 7, 14, 24, 34 © www.istockphoto.com/Heath Doman; p. 8 Jupiterimages/Comstock/Thinkstock; p. 11 © Stock Connection/SuperStock; p. 12 Glowimages/Getty Images; p. 13 (figure) © www.istockphoto.com/Max Delson Martins Santos, (measuring tape) © www.istockphoto.com/Zoran Kolundzija; pp. 14 (pigs), 17, 21, 25, 31, 41 © AP Images; p. 16 © Animals Animals/SuperStock; p. 22 Darren McCollester/Getty Images; p. 26 William Thomas Cain/Getty Images; p. 28 John A. Rizzo/Digital Vision/Getty Images; p. 29 Shutterstock.com; p. 35 Noel Hendrickson/Digital Vision/Thinkstock.

Designer: Nelson Sa; Editor: Kathy Kuhtz Campbell;
Photo Researcher: Karen Huang